Stem Cell Accelerator: Boost Stem Cells By 357% Naturally

Part 1: Supplementation for Stem Cells	3
Part 2: Intermittent Fasting for Stem Cells	4
INTRODUCTION	4
CHAPTER 1 - What Is The Feast and Famine Stem Cell Booster Diet?	6
CHAPTER 2 - THE BENEFITS OF THE FEAST & FAMINE DIET	8
CHAPTER 3 - GETTING YOURSELF READY TO BEGIN	10
CHAPTER 4 - COMMON BEGINNER MISTAKES	12
CHAPTER 5 - A SAMPLE FEAST DAY	14
CHAPTER 6 – A SAMPLE FAMINE DAY	16
CHAPTER 7 - SHOPPING GUIDELINES	18
CHAPTER 8 - INCORPORATING THE FEAST & FAMINE DIET INTO YOUR LIFESTYLE LONGTERM	20
CONCLUSION - TIPS TO BEGIN YOUR DIET JOURNEY TODAY	22
Part 3: Exercise for Stem Cells	24
Introduction:	24
How to Exercise: The Method	25
Stem Cell Accelerating Exercises	26
Workouts - How To Maximize Muscle Growth & Stem Cells	50
Part 4: Sleep for Stem Cells	51
Chapter 1 - Behavioral Changes for Healthy Sleep Habits	52
Chapter 2 - Self-Help Sleep Techniques	55
Chapter 3	67

Part 1: Supplementation for Stem Cells

Congratulations. This guide will give you a complete rundown on producing stem cells naturally. This will provide you a natural surge of stem cells which don't just help to increase your penis size. Let's start with the supplements that can help you.

There are two main supplements to take to boost your stem cell count.

They are Blue Green Algae and Vitamin D3. Take this Blue Green Algae supplement (click the link). This is the most important single step to increasing your stem cell count. When you combine this with high doses of Vitamin D3, you can begin to see vastly increased benefits of having a high stem cell count. The results will mean that you get faster, more effective enhancement.

Blue Green Algae, or Spirulina, creates the chain reaction that leads to stem cells in your body. In the main guide for the Penis Enlargement Remedy, you'll get an indication of how much to take, so be sure to read that guide from cover to cover to learn about how much you should take.

Now, let's move to something we didn't discuss in the Penis Enlargement Remedy book. Namely, the power of Vitamin D3. Most doctors always err on the side of caution with Vitamin D3 supplementation. However, this simply doesn't make sense.

When you consider that Vitamin D3 isn't a vitamin and that half an hour in sunlight will give you 25,000 UI of Vitamin D3, it's curious to wonder why doctors suggest tiny doses.

Vitamin D3 Dosages should be high!

Vitamin D3 is vitally important to your health. Humans who are low on Vitamin D3 tend to suffer from obesity, depression, arthritis and the common cold. Vitamin D3 is a mood enhancer and a health enhancer.

There is a theory that Jeff Bowles believes, which has been getting rave reviews on Amazon, in his book 'The Miraculous Results Of Extremely High Doses Of The Sunshine Hormone Vitamin D3 My Experiment With Huge Doses Of D3 From 25,000 To 50,000 To 100,000 Iu A Day Over A 1 Year Period'. He believes that an evolutionary quirk of ours is that we semi-hibernate. That means that when we don't have enough Vitamin D3 we gain weight (as food is about to be scarce) and our mood drops.

Vitamin D3 needs to be supplemented with Vitamin K2. I strongly recommend 40,000 UI of Vitamin D3 and a small amount of Vitamin K2. The reason we take Vitamin K2 is because it stops the build-up of calcium in the body. We recommend 2,500 mcg of Vitamin K2.

Part 2: Intermittent Fasting for Stem Cells

INTRODUCTION

Welcome to Part 2 of the Stem Cell Accelerator Program. This section is based on total health.

As you've probably guessed, a healthier body find it far easier to produce more stem cells. The more that are in your body, the easier and faster it will be to increase your penis size.

However, there's another huge benefit too. Your overall health will skyrocket when you use this diet. Think about it...

It's almost impossible to hide from the news and discussion about the obesity epidemic that's taking both lives and shattering the quality of life world wide. It's in the papers, on television and being blogged about on the internet almost endlessly.

If that's not enough, unless you're blind it's hard to walk the streets of any big city or small town and not see the end product of this epidemic first hand.

The hard brutal truth is that people are getting fatter and fatter and this is a real health crisis that only a fool could ignore.

There's plenty of reasons for this here are just the most blindingly apparent...

Many People Eat Way too Much Way too Often.

It's a hard truth that can't be escaped. The human body wasn't designed by nature to eat as much and as often as most people do. This packs on the flabby pounds as our bodies, which are machines that were designed for survival in not so great circumstances are pampered and overfed in a cushy and soft environment. Remove a bit of hunger from our lives and we will pack on fat and pack it on at lightning speed.

A Widespread Avoidance of Exercise.

After overeating the next huge issue is under exercising. Having less physical jobs as well as social lives that revolve around the digital rather than the physical once again takes our bodies away from what they were designed for: running, lifting, hunting and playing. The less muscle we carry the lower our metabolism which means even more fat is packed on. Do you see a pattern developing?

Lack of Quality Sleep.

The first two obesity builders contribute to the third. Poor diet and lack of exercise offer the fast track to broken sleep patterns which have been shown in more studies than can be counted to also wreck metabolism and pack on fat. Sleepless nights tossing and turning quickly equal an ugly spare tire of flab around the waist.

Medicine and Drugs

Coming along with our increasingly over medicated society are the side effects of all these medications, which commonly include weight gain and lethargy. Cultures who approach health more naturally and holistically have largely avoided this issue and have been also able to avoid the obesity related health concerns that come along with it. Our societies for the most part haven't figured this out yet.

These are just some of the many reasons the obesity plague is spreading in such a quick and deadly manner. There's plenty more, trust me.

The question stands - what can we do about it? How can we turn the tide against obesity?

The answer is, of course, diet and exercise. There's plenty of diverse ideas about both, some good and a few bad. This guide offers what I feel may be the perfect solution to a vast majority of people's struggle with putting on fat. It's fairly simple and packed with power, inline with both nature and common sense. Most importantly it works and works almost like magic.

It's called the Feast and Famine Stem Cell Booster Diet and it can change your life for the better. After reading this you will be armed with all you need to know about Feast and Famine to make it work and get the lean and healthy body of your dreams.

Get ready this is going to be a blast!

CHAPTER 1 - What Is The Feast and Famine Stem Cell Booster Diet?

The Feast and Famine Stem Cell Booster Diet may be new in name, but in practice has been with us for quite some time. What scientists have only very recently discovered is that this diet drastically increases the number of stem cells in your body too. When you combine this with the other sections in the Stem Cell Accelerator, you can increase your stem cell count, naturally, by 327%, meaning far faster increases to your penis size.

So, this is the latest tweak on an area of diet programs and ideas less catchingly referred to as Intermittent Fasting.

Intermittent Fasting is the rage in health, fitness and weight loss circles with it's ideas making it to publication and wide practice. It's popular because it works!

Here's the important guiding principles of Feast and Famine, what gives the diet its power. Try not to stray too far from this foundation if you expect to reap the full rewards of Feast and Famine...

Choose Your Fasting Schedule

There's two approaches generally. The first is alternating Feast days with Famine days, which is personally the method I have seen produce the best weight loss results. The second variant, and this is what you will see in intermittent fasting diets like the 5:2 Diet is to eat normally five days and fast two. Our Guide's information works well with both methods, although once again I prefer the first for best long term results as well as ease of use and likelihood of being able to stick with Feast and Famine.

Feasting Guidelines

There's not many. I suggest broadly not eating anything that's junk food or packed with empty calories especially if you are looking to burn off a lot of weight. This will also safeguard your overall health, which is important isn't it? Make sure you get in your fruit and vegetables, but don't be afraid to indulge without binge eating. The fact you have more food freedom at least half the time will make your Famine days much easier to manage psychology. And succeeding on any diet, Feast and Famine included, is 90% a mental game. In this mental dieting game no diet stacks the deck more in your favor than Feast and Famine.

Famine Guidelines

For those needing to drop serious pounds, 500 calories a day on Famine days is a good starting point. This can be adjusted as needed once your weight loss goals are met. Most Feast and Famine enthusiasts like to stay around this area to continue to both reap the health benefits of fasting and to also be able to maintain their Feasting freedom on their Feast days.

* Stay Hydrated. Fasting expert or if you have never fasted in any form before alike, I cannot stress enough the importance of staying hydrated. When your body detoxes on your Famine days and starts to move out some of the junk you have built up, it will go much smoother if you are drinking a proper amount of water. Ignore this advice and you may just experience some stomach pains, along with the lethargy and weakness that always comes with dehydration regardless of your diet plan.

One of the greatest strengths of intermittent fasting and the Feast and Famine Stem Cell Booster Diet is its simplicity. No diet logs, carbohydrate manipulation schemes and other complications. It works much more dramatically than diets that you need flow charts to follow too. If you can't stick to Feast and Famine it has nothing to do with being confused, but with a lack of will power, self discipline and most of all desire. I think you have those covered, don't you?

CHAPTER 2 - THE BENEFITS OF THE FEAST & FAMINE DIET

The Feast and Famine Stem Cell Booster Diet brings a load of benefits some more obvious than others. Are you ready to take a look? I think you'll find them really exciting. If radically reducing fat while also basking in these health benefits doesn't interest someone looking to transform their body for the better I'm not sure what will!

Natural Stem Cell Boost

The most obvious thing is that it radically boosts stem cell production in your body. Yet, there are so many other benefits that everyone should be using Intermittent Fasting...

Here are some more benefits.

Quickly Cut Body Fat Safely

This is why most people will explore the Feast and Famine approach to diet. You can expect to see the fat melt off as long as you take your Famine days seriously. Eat too much on those days and you are obviously missing the point. We know this works, we've seen it and now even better news - science backs it up!

Recent University of Illinois research has shown in those following alternate day reduced calorie plans (inline with our Guide's recommendations) lost significantly more fat than those eating normally and following the same exercise protocols. It's a plus to be on the right side of science when, sadly, they most often trail far behind the true health and diet vanguard!

Easy To Follow And Manage

The next ground breaking benefit of Feast and Famine is how easy it is to follow and manage. I've touched on this already, but it truly bears repeating. Anyone who has counted carbs on a ketogenic diet like Atkins or the many others I'm sure will quickly agree! Once you figure out in your head what your 500 or 600 calories on famine days looks like you are set. No calculators or complications, period.

Enhanced Mental Function

Yes, we suspected it, but science has backed us up again. Reduced weekly calories (which is what you get with the Feast and Famine Stem Cell Booster Diet) leads to increased focus, better memory and other enhanced cognitive function according to Mark Mattson's research for the Lancet. These effects may even carry over into the fight against Alzheimer's disease and other similar huge health concerns which Mattson is exploring further.

Improve Insulin Levels

One of the reasons why many people pack on and find it so hard to lose body fat is their out of whack insulin levels. The Feast and Famine approach optimizes insulin levels for healthy fat loss, which just adds to the amount of fat already being cut from the calorie reduction and heightened metabolism we've already touched on.

Frees Up Time On Famine Days

One of the surprise benefits of this approach is the new found time you find available on Famine days. Small meals and no constant snacking or grazing frees up a shocking amount of time and energy that can be used positively elsewhere. I've found, and others have confirmed this, that some of our most creative and productive days turn out again and again to be famine days! Far from not having energy you end up filled with it!

The Feast and Famine Stem Cell Booster Diet approach is packed with benefits, physical, mental and even social. It's hard to even think of anything, but a small drawback or two and then only for those who are lacking in the desire to "get lean" department. This is truly a method that changes lives for the best.

CHAPTER 3 - GETTING YOURSELF READY TO BEGIN

Any diet requires a bit of preparation at first, Feast and Famine is certainly not an exception. I will say it requires much less preparation by the nature of Feast and Famine than any other diet I can think of and you won't have to jump many hurdles, do any real expensive shopping or experience any of the other more traditional diet head aches.

Here's some tips to get yourself ready to get the most out our plan...

Read And Understand This Guide

It's pretty short so why not even read it twice. I've done my best to keep it fluff free and all the information and tips will make your journey at intermittent fasting Feast and Famine style much, much easier. If you like to read check out some of the books in our history chapter and you may find some other ideas you'd like to incorporate after you've done straight Feast and Famine for a bit.

If Possible At First Food Shop More Often

Here's a trick I used in the beginning days of my intermittent fasting experiments and I've suggested to many of my friends and clients who have given it high praise too. Only keep enough food on hand for the days needs. On Feasting days you will have the pleasure of picking out some new treat to indulge in and on Famine days you won't be as tempted to cheat than you would be if the refrigerator is packed with snacks. Now if you live rurally, or have a large family this may be less practical, but if you can do it I guarantee it will give you a big advantage over those who ignore this tip.

If You Skip A Day Just Get Right Back On Schedule

This diet is about freedom and abundance not restriction. If you have a family event, a date or even a slight slip up on a Famine day just get right back in action the next day and reduce your calories. No master dietary equations are fouled or other nonsense. Now don't make a habit of this or you may end up seeing less than optimal results, but once in a while is perfectly fine. This automatic leeway is built into the Feast and Famine program making it not a diet you can "fail" at if you stumble while getting into the groove, or any other time really!

Throw Out Your Past Diet Experiences

Feast and Famine requires a whole new view of dieting, so in all likelihood your past dieting experiences positive and especially negative don't offer a whole lot of relevance. I'd suggest you file them away and don't let them influence what you are doing here and now. This attitude, not only in dieting and fitness, but also in other areas of life can break chains and open up doors. See what you think.

Are you feeling more ready to begin? You should be because there's a bright, fit and happy new you waiting at the end of the Feast and Famine road. And it's a road not particularly long in most cases or even exceedingly difficult. You've taken the first step by reading this Guide, don't turn back now!

CHAPTER 4 - COMMON BEGINNER MISTAKES

Now just because the Feast and Famine Stem Cell Booster Diet is easy to understand and simple to apply to your lifestyle doesn't mean it's easy for all to practice or it's impossible to make mistakes. In fact some mistakes with intermittent fasting are fairly common among beginners, let's go over them and see if you can't avoid these pitfalls before you make them rather than after. A few of these I even learned the hard way!

Pigging Out on Too Much on Junk Food

Let's be serious for a second on the subject of getting lean and healthy. While we are allowed and encouraged to eat loosely and enjoyably on Feast days this doesn't mean we have a license to eat completely like a glutton. So if you are not losing weight the way you'd like to be and are eating endless chips, ice cream and candy on your Feast days tighten up your diet and eat healthier.

You should be striving to optimize your health anyway shouldn't you?

Being Scared to Death of Hunger

No one has ever starved to death eating 500 calories or less every other day. Nor have they damaged their body in any way. In fact, it's the opposite. You give your body time to replenish cells (vital for penis growth) instead of focusing energy on digesting food.

So if you are experiencing great stress and discomfort over being hungry every other day, it's time to gain more control over your mind. This is done by developing your will power doing things like following this diet even when you would rather not be, focusing on your desired end result. Be tough and be rewarded.

Eating Too Much On Famine Days

Let's not play games, 500 calories or less means 500 calories or less. If you are eating clean on your Feast days and still not losing weight it likely means you are eating too much on Famine days. Cut down what you are eating and if you must check the calorie counts to make sure you are at 500 calories or under.

Reducing Your Level of Activity

It's tempting for some to slow down their activities on Famine days. Don't fall into this. In fact with a little Feast and Famine experience under your belt you will realize Famine days actually free up more energy and you should strive to be even more active. Doing more is almost always better than doing nothing as long as you can do it safely.

Putting Yourself Unnecessarily Around People Who Don't Respect Your Diet Efforts.

Apart from close friends and family who it would be difficult to avoid, it's a downer to be around people who try to talk negatively about or discourage you from meeting your Feast and Famine goals. Again dieting is 90% mental so don't let other people mess with your mental game. It's annoying, defeatist and unnecessary!

These common beginner mistakes are all easy to avoid and if you stumble it's ok just keep going. The Feast and Famine Stem Cell Booster Diet has been designed to be both effective, open and user friendly. A little bit of self-reflection and you are quickly back on course and seizing the body and life of your dreams!

CHAPTER 5 - A SAMPLE FEAST DAY

The Feast and Famine Feast Day! Now comes the fun part, my friends! Let's dig deep into a sample Feast day while we are following the Feast and Famine Stem Cell Booster Diet.

This is taken from my own lifestyle and from a period of time when I was consistently losing weight as fast as I ever had every week without fail. My metabolism has never been superhuman either, so rest assured if this has worked for me it's very, very likely to work for you as well (with portion sizes adjusted if you are female, of course.)

Read on and enjoy. I hope it gets you filled with enthusiasm! You will notice I'm not including calories, because who counts calories on a Feast day?! I sure don't and you shouldn't either.

Breakfast

Breakfast is regarded by many nutrition experts as being the most important meal of the day. It's also a meal I've neglected most of my life due to the perils of enjoying sleeping in. Intermittent fasting has cleared that up - after a 500 calorie day I can't wait to really eat a substantial breakfast! I must say I feel much more ready for action after a full force breakfast.

4 Eggs Scrambled. I choose to go with whole eggs for hormonal optimization's sake, but often mix up the ways the eggs are prepared.

Fresh Tomato, Onion and Jalapeno Salsa. Extra hot and used as a condiment on top of my eggs.

4 pieces of Turkey Bacon. I will eat other styles of bacon when turkey bacon isn't available.

4oz of Steak Sauteed in Frying Pan. I only add this when I really want to indulge or if I feel like I need the extra protein for muscle building purposes.

8oz Milk. Whole milk is also great for guys looking to naturally boost their hormonal advantage.

Snack
A few hand fulls of Organic Almonds

Small Spinach Salad. I don't use dressing beyond olive oil and garlic and sometimes toss in some tomatoes, onion and cucumber depending what's on hand.

Lunch
Medium Baked Potato. I dress the potato with a bit of butter and garlic.

Two 6oz Grilled Chicken Breasts. Sometimes plain or sometimes with salsa on top if I have extra from breakfast.

Small Side of Mixed Vegetables. Snack
More Almonds!

Dinner

10oz Grilled Lean Steak. Plain beyond salt and pepper.

Small side salad or spinach salad.

Side Portion of White or Brown Rice.

As much Green Tea as I'd like to drink sweetened with pure stevia.

Occasionally a desert of organic sorbet, a small addiction of mine!

Snack

My after dinner snack is pretty wide open within reason. If I eat chips I make sure to not go overboard.

Vanilla Whey Protein shake made with half whole milk and half almond milk. I drink this right before bed.

This is just a sample Feast and Famine Feast day, but it should give you a great idea of what's possible when we eat smartly and abundantly. The real eye opener is when you eat like this half the time and still see the fat melting away. That's when you will become a full force Feast and Famine true believer!

CHAPTER 6 – A SAMPLE FAMINE DAY

Now after seeing a sample Feast and Famine Feast day it's time for a sample of the flip side - the all important Famine day where we will fast eating vastly reduced calories activating our metabolism, our "skinny gene" and setting ourselves up for both body transformation and all the other health benefits we have already discussed. This is again, from my own personal experience and the daily calorie total is focused on the magic number of 500 calories. I think you will find this a very manageable day that will hardly leave you suffering.

Pre-Breakfast
16oz Spring Water immediately upon wakening.

A cup of Fresh Coffee, no milk or cream sweetened with stevia. 0 calories.

Breakfast
A second cup of Fresh Coffee, no milk or cream

sweetened with stevia. 0 calories.

8oz Spring Water.

Now this doesn't seem like much of a breakfast, but I prefer to sleep in a bit and save my calories for lunch and dinner. This is my own personal choice and you may choose to distribute your calories differently if you are more of a morning person!

Snack
8oz Green Tea sweetened with stevia. 0 calories.
12oz Spring water.
Lunch
Finally time to get in some food, paying special intention NOT to over do it. This is the meal when many feel most tempted, since while eating a small dinner you know a large breakfast is coming up relatively quickly. Don't give in!

Two medium hard boiled eggs. Once again I like to make sure I eat whole eggs every day to maximize my hormonal optimization plan. You have the option of egg whites, egg beaters and so on. 175 Calories.

Two slices Whole Wheat Toast. Sometimes I eat the eggs on the toast and sometimes as a side depending on mood. 115 Calories.

A cup of Fresh Coffee, no milk or cream sweetened with stevia. 0 calories.

8oz spring water.

Total Lunch calories: 290 give or take.

Snack

8oz Green Tea sweetened with stevia. 0 calories. Yes, I do love caffeine on Famine day in case you were wondering. It serves to boost energy, raise metabolism and even acts as a mild appetite suppressant.

12oz Spring water. Dinner

Half a cup (after cooked) Spaghetti with a small amount of low fat / low calorie butter, salt, pepper and garlic. 150 calories.

One slice whole wheat toast. 55 calories.

12oz Spring Water.

Total calorie intake for the day roughly 495 calories. This puts right where we are hoping to be on a Famine day. I repeat these meals often since they are pretty much decision free and simple to prepare. They can also easily be ordered in all but the most incompetent of restaurants!

One last bit of advice - take a half hour on Sunday and figure out your five hundred calorie and below meals for the week rather than just trying to wing it and guess how many calories you are eating on Famine days on the fly. This will end up equating in much more weight loss over the long term and also save you a few head aches and a bit of possible confusion too. When in doubt repeat meals! Don't worry about getting bored a Feast day is less than 24 hours away!

CHAPTER 7 - SHOPPING GUIDELINES

Now that we hopefully have agreed that the Feast and Famine Stem Cell Booster Diet is more than do-able after looking at a sample Feast day and a sample Famine day I thought I'd share with you a few more intermittent fasting insider's secrets.

The fine art of shopping while following Feast and Famine. Although all of us develop our style of eating while on the diet which best suits our individual needs I've found having an experience veteran's shopping list can provide some helpful guidelines. So are you ready to go shopping Feast and Famine style? Let's do it!

Here's what we are packing our shopping cart with...

Non-hormonal Chicken Breasts. I'm a bit of a chicken addict and don't think I could live without it. I eat chicken at least once a day on Feast days, sometimes twice. I think of chicken as a sort of "neutral" protein that can be prepared in so many ways its wise to fall in love with.

Make sure the fat is trimmed off!

Non-hormonal Grass Fed Lean Beef. Another Feast day favorite, especially when I'm hitting it more heavily in the gym. When you are looking to put on muscle while cutting fat on Feast and Famine aim for around 1 gram of protein for every pound you weigh.

Eggs. As you've seen eggs are on the meal agenda often for both Feast and Famine days. Don't skip them, unless you are one of the few who can't stomach the thought of them!

A variety of Pasta. Organic Spinach

Organic Leaf Lettuce. I should add organic produce is not a must, but I try to stick with it when I can.

Tomatoes. Onions.

Miso soup. Miso soup is great for a change of pace on Famine days and has been shown in research to have all sorts of regenerative and health boosting qualities. Plus it tastes great too!

Green Tea. Essential. Green Tea is great for a extra fat burning boost, is inexpensive and calorie free.

Coffee. Spring Water.

Whey Protein. I've tried to avoid any supplement recommendations as the Feast and Famine Stem Cell Booster Diet works great without them, but a good protein shake is the one exception. Keep your protein levels high and you will have no worries at all about losing muscle while cutting body fat.

Stevia. A all natural and calorie free sweetener which will make you forget sugar ever even existed. A true gift from above.

Almonds. A go to snack.

Now a look at this list reveals that avoiding overly processed and junk food isn't a bad idea and you can still really Feast without it. That way if you go a bit crazy at a friend's or eating out occasionally your body won't even notice it. Buying too many terrible food choices probably sends the wrong message to your subconscious and may set up many for binge eating and failure. Some intermittent fasting experts disagree, but this is what my own personal experience has revealed. After you move beyond the beginner stage feel free to experiment!

CHAPTER 8 - INCORPORATING THE FEAST & FAMINE DIET INTO YOUR LIFESTYLE LONGTERM

The only way to really lose weight and keep it off is to make the mental switch from thinking in terms of short term dieting to the more dynamic perspective of making lasting healthy lifestyle choices.

Feast and Famine is the perfect tool to help you make that change. In fact after studying and experimenting with every major diet of the last decade, I can honestly say none in my opinion are better suited for a long term lifestyle choice than intermittent fasting and Feast and Famine. It's easy to manage, inexpensive to follow, relatively pleasant and enjoyable and very, very powerful. This covers nearly every category of a dream long term eating plan check list I can think of!

Here's some tips in incorporating Feast and Famine into your lifestyle long term...

Celebrate Your Successes With Feast And Famine.

Thinking positive and choosing to focus on the positive changes you have made while intermittent fasting will go a long way in solidifying it as a part of your lasting lifestyle. Try your best to not dwell on any poor weeks or bumps in the road you may experience. This will pay off huge dividends both in weight loss and in life. Again 90% of the game is mental, let's not forget.

Recruit Those Closest To You To Lend A Hand

Making your significant other close friends and family aware of how Feast and Famine works and letting them know you could use their help encouraging you to be disciplined on Famine days will help this healthy lifestyle really cement itself in place. Some may even choose to take up the Feast and Famine flag themselves when they see how great you look and feel. That's when you know you are really onto something!

Take Off A Week Off Every Few Months

Everyone needs a vacation occasionally. This will prevent burn out and give yourself a great pat on the back after months of discipline. If you can time your vacation from Feast and Famine with a real vacation from work or school even better! I've found a week off really helps recharge enthusiasm's batteries and allows me to plunge back into the Feast and Famine lifestyle full force.

Keep Expanding Your Knowledge Of Intermittent Fasting

A final way to make sure you stick with Feast and Famine as a lifestyle choice is to keep your brain engaged in learning new knowledge about intermittent fasting in all its forms. Join some forums, follow the news and the blogs and if you go to a gym make friends with others living this way of life. This will continually confirm what you are doing is both healthy and a good choice. It's always a good idea to have as big a support circle as possible.

Even if you take up Feast and Famine to lose some weight quickly planning to go back to your old ways of eating, let me warn you, you may very well end up hooked and sticking around for the duration. The good news is your body will be much healthier and look much better for your efforts. Breaking from the norm into a lifestyle that gets the most out of body and mind is a benefit that's priceless. Embrace it!

CONCLUSION - TIPS TO BEGIN YOUR DIET JOURNEY TODAY

Thanks for taking the time to read our Guide and I truly hope you have found it helpful and eye opening. I have no doubt if you throw your focus into the Feast and Famine Stem Cell Booster Diet you will achieve your weight loss goals and much more.

That said when do you plan to start? If you just hesitated you may be experiencing the greatest foe of achieving the body of your dreams of them all - the evil called procrastination. Before I leave let me share with you some tips that can help you slay that beast and begin your own transformation story today!

Just Do It

The Feast and Famine Stem Cell Booster Diet requires no special food, no supplements and no information, really, beyond this Guide to work and work well. So what are you waiting for? Start Feast and Famine right NOW. The only thing stopping you is your own inertia. Banish any thoughts of tomorrow or next week. Once again make a decision and start NOW.

Expose Your Excuses

Do you have reoccurring excuses why you can't start intermittent fasting today? Say these excuses out loud so you can hear how ridiculously self defeating they are. If you are still in doubt write them down and burn them as you free yourself from limiting beliefs.

Look At Yourself Naked In The Mirror.

If you are fat the mirror and a lack of clothes won't lie. Remind yourself your body won't change into something more pleasing until you first make a decision to change it and then second move forward with action in support of that decision. That action is to wisely adopt the Feast and Famine Stem Cell Booster Diet. If not you will likely look the same, if not worse, than you did in the mirror in the days, weeks, months and years to come. This may sound harsh, but a harsh truth is much better than a pleasant falsehood.

Quit Time Wasters.

Do you need so much social media, television or playing video games when your body isn't where you desire it to be? Are you putting the easy and distracting before the vital and important? If so why? Break the trance, quit the time wasters and build the new you NOW!

Write Your Goals Down As Clearly And Detailed As Possible.

There's a certain magic about the written word, especially when it comes to setting and achieving goals. This magic is even more pronounced when the written words are your own. Write down your goals big and small, read them and embrace Feast and Famine as a means to carry you in the direction you need to be headed. There isn't a success coach or sports psychologist alive who would argue against that advice! You shouldn't either.

Are you psyched about moving forward with Feast and Famine? I knew you would be. This could be a day you look back on decades from now and say "that's where I committed to serious life enhancing change!" The things offered by this lifestyle are just that serious. I'd love to hear your success story so please stay strong and in touch!

Part 3: Exercise for Stem Cells

Introduction:

In Part 3, we're concerned about exercises to improve the number of stem cells in your body. Before we get into specific exercises, I'm going to give you some weight lifting dogma. Rest is vitally important (Part 4 is all about sleep).

Isolation or Compound Exercises – How do You Decide?

Before deciding on what types of weight lifting exercises to do, it helps to have an understanding of the definitions of isolation versus compound exercises.

Isolation exercises, in the simplest of definitions, involve only one joint, and one muscle or muscle group. A very good example of this is the biceps curl. They are used by weight lifters to add detail to their muscles.

Of course, some will argue that no matter what exercise you do, there is no *true* "isolation" exercise, as most movements involve other muscles acting as stabilizers.

Compound exercises, on the other hand, involve moving more than one joint and muscle group at a time. One example is the squat exercise, which involves your core, buttocks, lower back, and legs. A few other examples of compound exercises include lunges, chin-ups, and dead lifts.

In general, compound exercises are the recommended path to go at the start. Once you have achieved the physique you want, and want to improve particular muscles, then isolation exercises can be performed.

Here are 5 reasons to choose compound exercises over isolated exercises:

1. **You can spend less time lifting weights**

A lot of people complain that they do not have time to work out. Now, you have no excuses. If you can incorporate compound exercises into your routine, you will be working out more muscles and muscle groups in less time. You can get away with doing three to five exercises each time.

2. **You will still have time to do other exercise**

It is still important to ensure you do some cardiovascular exercise, and then spend some time stretching out when your muscles are still warm to help improve your range of motion and flexibility.

3. **You burn more calories**

By employing more than one muscle group, your body rewards you by using up more calories.

4. **You will see results quicker**

Let's face it. When you start to see results, it keeps you motivated and progressing towards your goals. By focusing on multiple muscles and muscle groups, you will see the transformation in your physique more quickly.

5. **Compound exercises cause your body to release more hormones INCLUDING STEM CELLS**

You should notice that performing compound lower body workouts (i.e. your legs) will result in a harder workout than just doing your biceps, for example. The harder the workout is, the more hormones get released into your body. Human growth hormone (HGH) is one of those hormones. It has a number of functions including maintaining your blood sugars within normal levels, and increasing your body's ability to break down fat. It is also important in the growth of muscle. You will get the most results by lifting more weight, and reducing your rest time between sets.

How to Exercise: The Method

Why does your body grow. The answer is really simple. It grows and adapts mainly out of subconscious fear.

Lemme explain…

Say you push yourself further than you've ever been pushed before. There are two possibilities here: 1, You're avoiding danger. i.e. A lion chased you and you nearly didn't make it. The message to your body here is that you have to adapt, or next time you might get caught.

2, You nearly starved. You are exerting all this energy to get food. Therefore, to make killing an animal easier, you get stronger or faster to get it.

Your body wants a life that's as easy as possible. So it's only when pushed to the extremes that you adapt.

Bearing that in mind, the way to boost stem cells (and testosterone) is to exercise so that your body is continually forced to adapt. This means that every time you go into the gym you need to improve on your previous performance. Doing this will make your body keep getting bigger, better and more efficient.

Not only will you look better, you'll also experience much faster penis enlargement.

I want you to either buy a notebook or use something on your phone to record every exercise, every rep and what weight it was all at.

Once you have that information, you'll be able to beat your previous best every single time. Now, this leads to your body being forced to flood stem cells into you at a very high rate. When this is done you know that getting bigger will be faster and you'll see bigger gains.

Yet, you'll also look and feel like a million dollars. Ladies will eye you up, you'll be better in bed and you'll be more of a catch.

Now we're going to see what exercises are the most effective to dramatically boost your stem cells.

Stem Cell Accelerating Exercises

1, Chest & Arms
Barbell Bench Press

1. Lie on your back on the bench.
2. Grasp the barbell approximately shoulder width apart.
3. Lower the barbell towards your chest while bending elbows and keeping them close to your body.
4. Push barbell back up by straightening your elbows.
5. Then lower barbell back down towards your chest, and then repeat according to the number of repetitions you are doing.

Tips for this exercise:
- Important: Use a spotter (someone who can stand by and assist as needed)
- You can adjust the incline of the bench from flat to incline, depending

This exercise works your arms (triceps) and your chest at the same time.

2, Biceps Curls

1. Stand relaxed with your feet shoulder width apart, and knees slightly bent.
2. Hold dumbbells in both hands.
3. Keeping your elbows close to your body and your shoulders down, gently bend both elbows, lifting the weights towards your shoulders as you do so.
4. Slowly lower both dumbbells back to their original positions.

Tips for this exercise:

- Don't drop the weights back down to your sides. Use controlled movement and descent.
- You can also do this exercise by alternating arms, instead of moving both at the same time.

Biceps curls are an isolation exercise for your biceps brachii muscles.

3, Decline Barbell Triceps Extensions

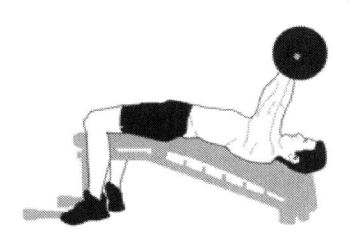

1. Lie on the decline bench.
2. Hold the barbell with a narrow grip (hands close together).
3. Begin with the barbell held above your shoulders with your elbows straightened.
4. Now lower the barbell by bending your elbows.
5. The bar will go overhead and clear your head.
6. Straighten your elbows, and bring the barbell back to its original position located above your shoulders.

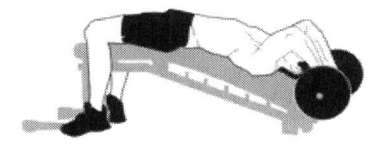

This exercise targets your triceps muscles located on the back of your arms. These muscles are responsible for straightening your elbows.

4, Dips

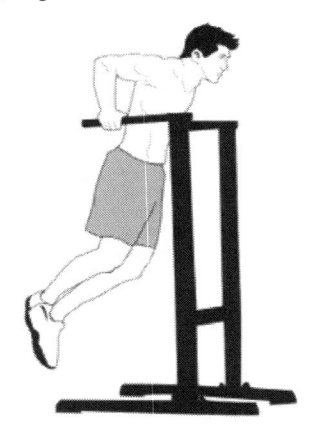

1. Grasp dip bar with both hands.
2. Bend your hips and knees a bit.
3. Lift yourself up by straightening your elbows.
4. Your shoulders will end up above your hands.
5. Lower yourself back down by bending your elbows.
6. Raise yourself back up with straight arms, and repeat according to the number of repetitions you are doing.

Tips for this exercise:

- As you get better at this exercise, you can increase its difficulty by adding weight (dumbbell) between your ankles.

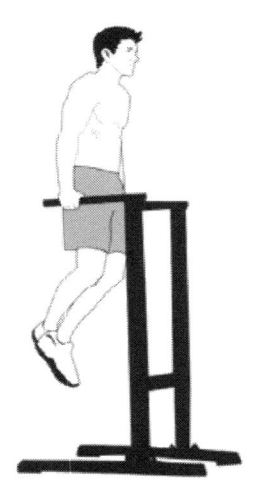

This is a compound exercise that works your arms and chest muscles.

5, Dumbbell Bench Press

1. Lie down on the bench
2. Put a dumbbell in each of your hands
3. Place your feet flat on the floor
4. Push the dumbbells up as seen in the picture, with your palms facing away from you.
5. Tuck your chin in.
6. Lower the dumbbells down, and bring your elbows down a bit lower than your shoulders.
7. Then lift the dumbbells back up again.

Tips for this exercise:

- Tighten your abdominals
- Ensure your back is not flattened against the bench (see first picture)
- Do not lock your elbows when lifting the dumbbells.
- Keep your shoulders on the bench.

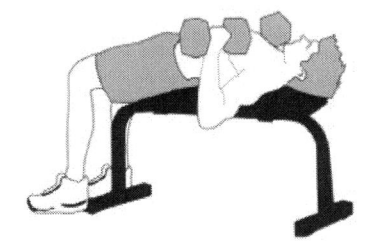

This exercise will work your chest, as well as your shoulders and triceps.

6, Push-up Rows

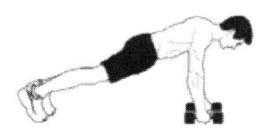

1. Place 2 dumbbells about shoulder width apart.
2. Get into the position like you see in the first image, with arms straightened.
3. Slowly lower yourself down like when you are doing a regular push-up (image 2).
4. Pause, and then bring yourself back into the first position.
5. Repeat as much as you can. Increase repetitions as you progress.

Tips for this exercise:

- Once you've mastered this, you can add more challenge by "rowing the dumbbell." In order to do this, when you come back to the original position (first image), you lift one dumbbell up. Then do another push up, and then lift the other dumbbell up. There are several

This exercise works your chest, arms, back, and core.

2, Core & Lower Back Exercises
Decline Plank Position

1. Place your feet on a workout bench as shown in the image above.
2. Then get into plank position with your elbows resting at 90 degrees on the floor.
3. Hold for as long as you can.
4. Repeat, and hold for as long as you can again.
5. Challenge yourself to increase the length of time and number of reps you can do.

This is another variation of the plank position, one of the best core/abdominal exercises you will ever do. Not only does it work your core, it also works your hip and lower back muscles.

2, Hip Raises with a Swiss Ball

1. Begin by lying down on your back on the floor.
2. Place your feet on top of the Swiss ball with your knees slightly bent (first picture).
3. Extend/straighten your hips to lift your buttocks off the floor (second picture).
4. Continue to lift your buttocks off the floor so that your knees are bent to a 90 degree angle (third picture).
5. Slowly lower yourself back to original

This exercise works out your core and lower back.

3, Oblique Crunches with Swiss Ball

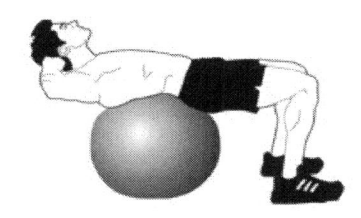

1. Lie down on the Swiss ball with your knees bent to 90 degrees, feet flat on the floor, and your arms behind your head (as in top image)
2. Then lift your trunk up and off the ball.
3. Keeping your arms and elbows in place, bring your left elbow down to your right knee (as shown in bottom image).
4. Lie back down (as you see in the top image).
5. Now, sit back up as in the bottom image.
6. This time, move your right elbow towards your left knee.

This exercise will work your abdominals and lower back muscles.

4. **Plank Position on a Swiss Ball**

1. Kneel on the floor in front of the ball.
2. Place your elbows on the ball, as shown in the image above.
3. Slowly get to your feet, and straighten out your hips and back as shown above.
4. Hold for as long as possible.
5. Repeat as many times as desired.

This exercise is another variation of the regular plank exercise, where you are in the above position, only without the Swiss ball and you are on the floor.

Although it looks easy, it is one of the best ways to strengthen your core muscles.

The above exercise can add some challenge to doing the regular

5, Side Plank

Begin the side plank position, as shown in Figure 1 below. You are working out your abdominals, hip muscles, and lower back muscles.

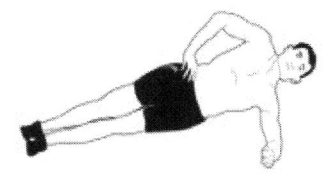

Figure 1

Once you want more of a challenge, you can add the elbow touches to the floor, while remaining in a side plank position (as in Figure 2 below).

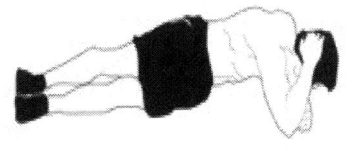

Figure 2

This side plank position will work various abdominals, hips, and lower back muscles.

3, Shoulder & Back Exercises
1, Dumbbell Incline Row

1. Lie face down on an incline bench.
2. Hold dumbbells in each hand, with palms facing inward, and arms and elbows straight (first picture).
3. Squeeze your shoulder blades together, and bend your elbows to bring the dumbbells up (second picture).
4. Lower the dumbbells back to their original position.

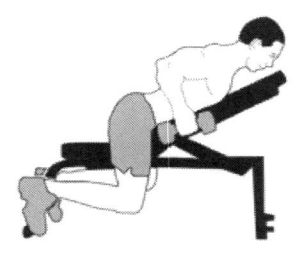

This is a great beginner compound exercise that works the muscles of your middle back, as well as your shoulders, biceps,

2, Dumbbell Push Press

1. Stand with your elbows bent holding the dumbbells just above your shoulders, as shown in the top picture. Palms should be facing inwards.
2. Feet should be shoulder width apart.
3. Bend your knees (as you see in the middle/second photo).
4. Push the dumbbells above your head forcefully, using your legs to help propel you (as shown in the bottom/third photo).
5. Completely straighten your elbows above your head.
6. Lower the dumbbells back to the original position (as shown in the first picture).
7. Continue to repeat.

This is a compound exercise that works your shoulders, while also using other muscles such as your quadriceps, hamstrings, gluteals, and triceps.

3, Inverted Row

You may hear this exercise also referred to as the horizontal barbell pull-up

1. Place a barbell bar in the rack at approximately waist level.
2. Position yourself **underneath** the bar.
3. Hold onto the bar slightly wider than shoulder-width apart.
4. Ensure your arms are straight, your heels are resting on the floor, and your body is angled under the bar.
5. Squeeze your shoulder blades together.
6. Bend your elbows, thereby moving your chest toward the bar.
7. Then return your body back to its original position with straight arms.
8. Repeat the movement.

This is a compound exercise that works your back muscles (middle back and latissimus dorsi).

4, Seated Dumbbell Curl to Shoulder Press

1. Sit on a workout bench. Hold dumbbells in each hand, with your palms facing forwards. Your elbows/arms should be straight (first picture).
2. Bend your elbows, bringing the dumbbells towards your shoulders (second picture).
3. Turn your forearms so your palms will face **forwards.**
4. Then lift the weights above your head as you straighten your arms (as shown in third picture).
5. Lower your arms back down (as in second picture).
6. Bring your arms back to their original positions (first picture).

This compound exercise will work your shoulders and your biceps.

5,

Shoulder Fly on Incline

1. With dumbbells in hand, lie prone (face down) on an incline bench.
2. Flex your elbows to 90 degrees as shown in the first picture, with your palms facing upwards.
3. Keeping elbows bent to 90 degrees, lift both your arms/dumbbells while you bring your shoulder blades together (as shown in second picture).
4. Then gradually lower your arms back to the original position you started from.

Tips for this exercise:

- As you progress, putting the bench in less incline can add challenge and work different muscles.

This exercise works your shoulder muscles, your trapezius (the muscle that runs from the back of your skull down your back to your lower thoracic vertebrae), and your rhomboids (muscles found between your scapulae/shoulder blades that allow you to squeeze them together).

6. Single Arm Dumbbell Row

1. Stand bent at waist with your back flat (as shown in the picture) with dumbbell in one hand. Place your free hand behind your back, **or** place it on your knee (on the side opposite the arm holding the dumbbell).
2. Make sure your feet are far apart, approximately hip width apart.
3. Feet should be flat on the floor, and ensure that your leg (on the same side as the hand holding the dumbbell) is slightly behind the other foot.
4. Bend your elbow to lift the dumbbell up, so that your upper arm is parallel with the floor (second picture).
5. Return your arm to the original position, and continue repetitions.

Tips for this exercise:

- Lift the weight with controlled ascent.
- Focus on using your back muscles.
- Pull your shoulders and scapulae (shoulder blades) back.
- A variation of this exercise is to use a bench, and support your

This is a compound exercise working your back, shoulders, and biceps.

4, Legs
1, Barbell Dead Lifts

1. Place your feet below the bar.
2. Bend down by bending your knees.
3. Places your hands on the bar, about shoulder width apart (first picture).
4. Lift the barbell by straightening your knees and hips (second picture).
5. Keep arms straight during lift.
6. Pull your shoulders back slightly when standing.
7. Lower barbell while keeping arms straight.

Tips for this exercise:

Ask a personal trainer for advice on

A dead lift is a great compound exercise that targets many muscles including gluteals, quadriceps, hamstrings, your back, trapezius, and forearm muscles.

2, Dumbbell Squats

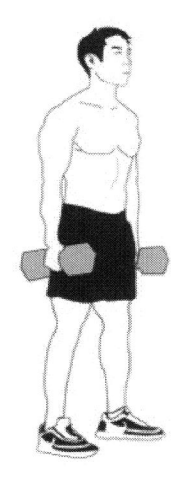

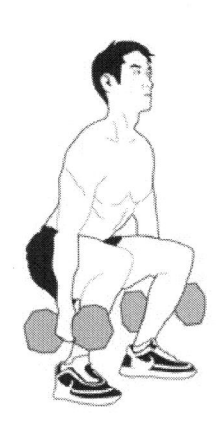

1. Begin with dumbbells in hand, and arms straight at your side. Palms are facing inwards (first picture).
2. Lower yourself down slowly by bending your knees. Your knees should not come in front of your feet. Imagine you are sitting on an invisible chair. Pause.
3. Raise yourself back up to the original position.
4. Continue repeating.

Tips for this exercise:

- When you are just beginning, you may want to make this a true bodyweight exercise, and exclude the weights. You can add weights as you progress.
- Aim to get your thighs parallel with the floor.

3, Front Squats with Barbell

1. Use a barbell that is on the floor or one on a rack
2. Grasp the barbell in your hands (see picture of hand position).
3. Hands should be placed slightly wider than shoulder width apart.
4. The bar should be placed in front of your shoulders, and your elbows should be forwards (as in picture). Your hands should be relaxed, as shown.
5. Turn feet slightly outwards (approximately 35 degrees). Your feet should be hip width apart for stability.
6. Lower yourself to the ground with the barbell, bending your hips as though you are sitting down. Your knees should stay behind your toes.
7. Aim to get your thighs parallel and level with the floor.
8. Stand back up with controlled ascent.
9. Repeat the movements.

Tips for this exercise:
- Remember that your shoulders are supporting the weight, not your hands.
- Look forwards, not up.
- Have a spotter present for safety.

This is a compound exercise that works your leg muscles (quadriceps and hamstrings), and gluteal muscles.

4. **Lunges (shown with dumbbells)**

1. Stand with your arms by your side, holding the dumbbells. Your palms are facing inwards as you see in the first picture.
2. Move one leg ahead of the other.
3. Lower your body down by bending your knees.
4. Keep your trunk upright.
5. Make sure that the front leg's knee (as you see in the second picture) stays behind your toes. In other words, your knee should not extend past your foot.
6. Push yourself back up to return to the original standing position.
7. Continue to perform repetitions with that same leg, and then alternate legs so that both legs get a workout. The other option is to alternate legs throughout the exercise, ensuring both legs get a workout.

Tips for this exercise:

- If you are a beginner, you do not need to use the dumbbell weights at the start.
- As you progress, you may want to try this exercise out with barbells.
- Another variation of this exercise is to move across the room doing "walking lunges."

5, Single Leg Squat

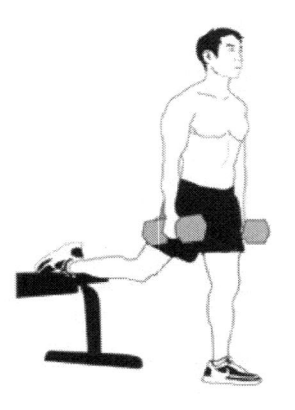

1. Stand facing away from the bench, with dumbbells in your hands.
2. Extend your hip back, as shown in the picture, and put your foot on the bench.
3. Lower yourself down by bending at the knee and hip, until your knee almost makes contact with the floor.
4. Then stand back up.
5. Repeat this motion, according to the number of repetitions you are doing.
6. Alternate legs, and follow the same instructions.

Tips for this exercise:

- Make sure your knee points in the same direction as the foot you have on the floor.
- If it is too hard to do this exercise with dumbbells, you can modify it to a body-weight exercise only where you don't use dumbbells until later.
- This exercise can also be modified to be done with a barbell. Ask a professional for advice on how to do this.

6. Split Squats with Dumbbells

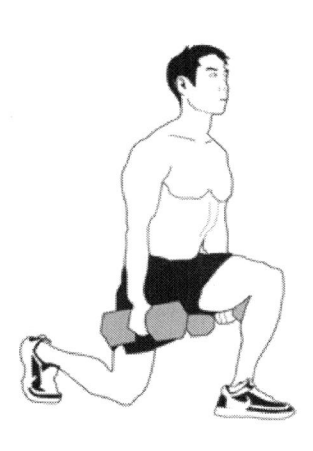

1. Stand with one leg in front of the other, as shown in the picture.
2. Have dumbbells in your hands.
3. Lower yourself down by bending the hip and knee of the front leg.
4. The heel of your back foot will come off the floor during this exercise.
5. Continue to lower yourself down so that your back leg almost touches the floor.
6. Stand back up to starting position.
7. Continue to repeat for number of repetitions you are doing.
8. Then alternate legs so you can exercise your other leg.

Tips for this exercise:

- Make sure your front knee and foot are pointed in the same direction.
- Adjust amount of weight to

Workouts - How To Maximize Muscle Growth & Stem Cells

When you work out, make a day in the gym for each section. i.e. Legs is one day's worth of exercise.

On that day, you need to train to failure on all exercises. That means, to the point where you're incapable of doing another repetition. Once you've trained to failure, your job is done. Don't do another repetition of that exercise.

Reaching failure is the goal.

The way to do this is to do 10 reps, raise the weight, 10 more reps, raise the weight and then do as many reps as you can until you fail. Now, the weights should always be staggered, and on the last set of repetitions you should be able to do between 5 and 15.

Also, the amount of weight that you add each time isn't a lot. You should start heavy and lift heavy. Once you can achieve 20 reps at the highest weight, you raise all the weights for the next time in the gym on that exercise.

That's how you produce lots of muscle growth, stem cells and hGH in the body.

Part 4: Sleep for Stem Cells

Everyone experiences trouble sleeping once in a while. While this may be inconvenient, it's often temporary. When occasional sleepless nights turn into a regular occurrence of many nights in a row with interrupted sleep, you might have a sleeping problem. And sleeping problems are bad for stem cell production...

When you don't get enough sleep for an extended period of time your tiredness impacts every part of your life. Physically, you might notice a decrease in your productivity and daily activities. Emotionally, you may experience relationship problems or a change in your personality. Mentally, a chronic sleep problem can create stress and anxiety.

There are three categories of sleep deprivation and insomnia. The first stage, called "initial" insomnia, is when you first realize you're having difficulty achieving a sleep state and occurs when it takes longer than a half an hour to fall asleep. "Middle" insomnia is when you have difficulty staying asleep. Once awakened, you stay awake through the wee hours of the morning. The most sever level of insomnia is "late" or "terminal" insomnia. This is when you wake up early in the morning and stay awake after sleeping less than 6 hours.

There are a variety of reasons that you may be having trouble sleeping. If your insomnia is due to a medical condition, your doctor will be able to provide you with suggestions and appropriate medical attention. If it's determined that your sleep problem is due to a medical condition, the condition will be treated with the intention that this will in turn treat the insomnia.

On the other hand, if your sleep difficulties are occurring because you are stuck in a cycle of sleepless nights, or your insomnia is due to your inability to reach a state of inner peace needed to achieve sleep, this book is for you. Here you'll find healthy options to try before taking potentially harmful and habit forming prescription sleep aids.

In this book you'll learn about:

- Preparing the perfect sleep environment
- Relaxation techniques

- The role of exercise and diet in your sleep health
- How to quiet your mind to promote good sleep
- Beneficial natural supplements

When following the tips in this book, you will have all of the tools needed to stop tossing and turning at night and start enjoying a full night's sleep, naturally. You will wake up feeling rejuvenated and attentive, instead of exhausted and restless. Prepare yourself drift off to dreamland naturally!

Chapter 1 - Behavioral Changes for Healthy Sleep Habits

Habits at Bedtime

It is essential that your brain has consistency by creating a bedtime schedule so that your body can learn how to fall asleep without medication. Create a sleep strategy to determine the best routine, and plan to follow the routine for one to two weeks before making any alterations.

Your sleep strategy should include:

- A regular bedtime
- A consistent wake time
- A record of any natural supplements you have tried
- Routine activities that are not stimulating such as brushing your teeth or reading

Moving through a regular bedtime process will signal to your brain that it's time to go to sleep. The desired end result of having a sleep strategy is regular sleep that's restful and refreshing.

Plan to get 7-8 hours of sleep nightly, and don't allow yourself to oversleep. If you wake up the same time every day you'll establish a routine. Avoid naps during the day because your body will be confused, and it will interrupt your sleep pattern. You can't bank extra hours of sleep, and trying to sleep later in the morning to make up for sleep lost overnight will leave you feeling tired.

Every person has different sleep habits, so be patient while you work through the process of finding the sleep plan that works best for you.

Sleep Environment

In addition to a regular bedtime schedule, it is important to make you bedroom a place that is conducive to sleep. The more comfortable and relaxing your sleep space is, the better your chances for falling asleep and staying asleep. Consider these tips when creating your relaxing sleep atmosphere:

- Get rid of all annoyances and interruptions.
- Control the room temperature; cooler air (between 65 and 70 degrees F) is typically more comfortable for sleep, however, set the temperature to your preference.
- Allow for room ventilation, if possible. Crack a window slightly to allow for air flow. The circulating fresh air will help you breathe deeply, and provide oxygen that is essential for good sleep.
- Use ear plugs if there are noises outside the bedroom. There are many types of plugs that are specifically for sleeping, so if at first you don't find the perfect pair, try another.
- Mask noises with a white noise machine if you decide to not wear earplugs. Machines are designed specifically for this purpose, or you can use a fan or air conditioner to provide the background noise. This will hide background sounds such as traffic or a barking dog.
- Try using a CD player to play soothing background music.
- Your circadian rhythm, your body's internal clock, relies on light and dark patterns to determine when to signal your body to fall asleep. Keep your room as dark as possible to help your body settle into a sleep state. Use mini-blinds and thick curtains to block light from windows. Try wearing an eye mask to block any remaining light.
- Having a clock by your bedside might be adding to your sleep problem. If you are watching the clock all night long, face it toward the wall so that you can't see the time. Constantly looking at the clock only makes you think about sleep, and lack of sleep, which continues the cycle of sleeplessness.

- Consider a room humidifier for winter months when the air is dry.
- Use your room only for sleeping. Remove the TV, computer, stereo. Your mind should associate your bedroom only with sleep.
- Wear the most comfortable clothing you own. Non-constrictive clothing won't wake you in the middle of the night.

As you can see here, there are many different tips to try to help you sleep better. Each individual has their own unique combination of elements that make up their perfect sleep environment. If one suggestion doesn't work for you, make note and try another until you find out what works best for you.

Sleep Equipment

Also important to the sleep environment is the equipment used when sleeping. Sleep equipment includes the pillow, bedding, mattress, and sleep clothes.

Your mattress should be smooth and firm so that your back is well-supported and your body is comfortable when lying down. Make sure the mattress is supported completely by the bed frame to avoid sagging.

The mattress should also be appropriately sized for your body. Make sure you have a big enough bed so that you have enough space. If you have a single or double bed, consider buying a larger queen or king sized mattress.

Use whatever style and type of pillow you find most comfortable. It doesn't matter what it's made of as long as it provides you with neck and head support.

The sheets and blankets should be clean and pressed. If you do not like feeling tucked in, loosen the sheets so that your feet can move around freely.

To find the right temperature for you, experiment with different blankets of a variety of weights and materials. Since a cool room is most conducive to sleep, keep the lower temperature in mind when selecting bedding.

Find a sleep position that is comfortable for you and lay in that position so that your body knows it's time for sleep. Whether it is lying on your back, on your side, or on your stomach, your favorite position will help you instantly get relaxed.

Chapter 2 - Self-Help Sleep Techniques

Color Therapy

Using color therapy, or "chromatherapy", is a unique way to treat a variety of ailments, including, but not limited to, sleep problems. Chromatherapy involves being exposed to color in various ways. Being shown colored lights, visualizing and meditating on a color, being massaged with colored oils, and wearing specific colors can help treat both physically and emotionally caused sleep problems.

Chromatherapy has a long history. Ancient Indian beliefs practiced chromatherapy in Ayurvedic medicine, where it was believed that colors corresponded to parts of the body, emotions and spiritual aspects of life. They believed that each of the charkas, areas of energy in the body, linked to a color.

Ancient Egyptians used chromatherapy by breaking up the sunlight with specially created lenses. They built solariums where they practiced chromatherapy.

Chromatherapy as we know it was developed in the late 1600's when scientist Sir Isaac Newton proved that light is a mixture of color from the full range of color we can see.

Modern-day color therapy came about when Dr. Edwin D. Babbitt penned his Principles of Light and Color. In this publication he outlined how color therapy could be used to treat a variety of maladies, include sleep difficulties.

The 1940's were a time of experimentation with color therapy. During this time, Russian scientist S.V. Krakov experimented with chromatherapy and determined that when he separated light spectrum's wavelengths it had an impact on the nervous system. For example, he found that red light increased blood pressure and impacted the adrenal glands. White light and blue light were found to be relaxing. This groundbreaking information is still used today by color therapy practitioners.

How does it color therapy work? Color is a part of what makes up light, and light has many different energy waves. When light enters the retina of the eye, it touches the photoreceptor cells in the eye. The photoreceptors turn the light into electrical impulses, which signal the brain to release hormones. By controlling the release of hormones, chromatherapy can be used to treat insomnia and other sleep-related difficulties.

In a time when alternative medicine is becoming more popular, Chromatherapy is actively being used by the medical community to treat disorders such as depression and seasonal affective disorder (SAD).

Some types of color therapy should only be practiced by trained professionals. However, there are color therapy techniques that can be practices safely at home.

To try chromatheraphy on your own, follow these tips. Select hues to wear based on your recommended color. When eating, choose foods that are a particular color. Spend time visualizing a recommended color.

Be aware of the following potential concerns:

- Never replace traditional care with chromatherapy for severe insomnia.
- Epileptics should avoid looking directly at any type of flashing lights.
- When using colored lights, do not look directly into the light. Receive colored light therapy indirectly by looking at an object that is lit by the colored light.
- If you are on prescription medication, check the label for a light sensitivity side effect. Exposure to bright light might cause a problem.

Physical Activity

Getting exercise during the day is an important factor in how well you sleep at night. If you are physically active during the day, you body will be able to relax and fall asleep easier. Exercise helps your body deal with daily stress and anxiety. It impacts the chemicals in your brain, and how much you exercise is directly linked to your physical and emotional health. Regular exercise will help you fall asleep and maintain a sleep state because your sleep cycles become more consistent and the transition between them becomes more seamless. Try to work exercise into your life daily to avoid sleeplessness.

When getting physical activity, plan to exercise more than 3-4 hours before bedtime. For the best sleep benefit, be physically active in the late afternoon or early evening.

Try to be physically active for at least 20-30 minutes a day, 3-4 times per week. Aerobic activities usually work best to remedy insomnia, and activities can range from an easy walk to a rigorous run. By making your heart rate go up, improving your lung capacity, and adding oxygen into your blood, your body will be in better health and you'll be on your way to naturally correcting your sleep problem.

In addition to aerobic exercise, there are other types of physical activity you can do to fight sleeplessness. Consider yoga or Tai Chi. Yoga affects the brain and core muscles and improves blood circulation. Using yogic breathing techniques will help you relax and live with less stress. Tai Chi incorporates breathing with body movements in a slow-moving style that is perfect for individuals with joint pain or other issues that keep you from high-impact exercise.

If adding 30 minutes of exercise into your daily schedule is too tough, try adding small blocks of physical activity. Making small changes, like taking the stairs instead of the elevator, or purposely parking further away from your destination will help you live a healthy, energetic life.

Relaxation through Meditation

It only stands to reason that the more relaxed you are the more likely you are to fall asleep and maintain a satisfactory sleep state. It's essential to quiet your mind in order to fall asleep quickly. By using meditation you can stop thinking, worrying, or what ever else is going through your head.

There are several different meditation and visualization methods that will help you relax. Try one of these meditation styles:

1. Focal point method. Select a focal point, whether it is a mantra, visual point, or even your own breathing. A mantra is a word or phase that is repeated either in your mind or out loud to help you focus on meditating. The use of a mantra or other focal point will help keep you on track and keep your mind from wandering. You need to be disciplined to practice this method of meditation, because thoughts will come into your head and you will be tempted to think about other things. This method will become easier the more you practice it.

2. Breathing-focused meditation. Find a comfortable, quiet space and sit on the floor, using a cushion if so desired. Sitting with your hands in your lap, calm your body and close your eyes. Breathe in and out through your nose. Make an effort to concentrate on your breathing, counting each breath in and out until you reach ten. Continue counting in groups of ten until you begin to feel relaxed. Empty your mind of everything and concentrate only on counting as you inhale and exhale. If thoughts enter your mind, acknowledge that they are there and let them go, again focusing on your breath. When you have finished meditating, become aware of your body once more and stretch before getting up.

3. Guided imagery. This method combines visualization with meditation and hypnosis. This type of meditation is guided, and you are led to visualize relaxation, which helps you feel relaxed. Find a place that is quiet and dimly lit. Using a tape or CD player, play a pre-recorded imagery recording. Guided imagery usually starts with deep breathing and other deep breathing exercises. When you relax, your imagination comes alive and the recording will guide you through a variety of scenes, using your imagination to help you find peacefulness and relaxation. Common guided imagery scenarios include beach side strolls, mountain hikes, or nature walks through the forest. At the end of your guided imagery session you should feel calm and relaxed.

The aforementioned meditation methods are only a sampling of the wide array of choices available. Experiment with these, and research others, to find one that helps you fight insomnia.

Simple Respiration: Breathing and Relaxing

Breathing is the simplest and easiest way to find complete relaxation and stress reduction. The more deeply you breathe, the more serene you will become. These relaxation tips will help your body wind down and get ready for sleep.

When you first get into bed:

Lie down and breathe deeply through your nose. Imagine the air moving into your stomach. On your next inhale, breathe in for four counts. Exhale slowly through your pursed lips, while counting to eight. You will feel the tension leave your body with every exhale. Repeat this technique six to ten times for immediate relaxation. Practice deep breathing daily to develop a healthy habit of regular relaxation. Calming your mind will help you fall asleep.

Before going to bed try this relaxation technique:

Lie down with your back to the floor and your arms at your side, palms facing upward. Your feet should be comfortably apart. With your eyes closed, mentally concentrate on each part of your body, tensing then releasing each group of muscles. Starting at the top of your head, release tension as you move slowly down your body. Feel your forehead, eyes and mouth. Work through your shoulders, neck and back. Move down to your toes, then bask in the relaxed state you have achieved. Focus on your breathing, making sure breath is coming from your stomach. Breathe deeply and slowly, letting go of all your concerns and stress. When your body knows it's okay to let go of your worries and stressors, you'll be able to go to sleep naturally.

There are many other techniques for breathing and relaxation. Through your own experimentation and practice you can find one that works well for you.

Music and Sounds for Sleep Induction

Using noise as a tool to help fall asleep has been done since the beginning of time. The earliest form of this technique is the lullaby, which has successful soothed even the most colicky baby. There are many CDs and sound devices on the market today that are designed to have the same effect as a mother singing or humming a child to sleep. Here are a few suggestions:

- Relaxing classical music CDs or tapes are a wonderful way to relax and put your mind at ease. Look for "Baroque Music" by Mozart, "Lullaby" by Brahms, and "Waltzes" by Strauss. This is only a small sampling of the many, selections available.

- Try something soothing and modern. Ambient Electronica, which is also called "downtempo" and "chillout", is a great way to unwind. Gently mixing an ongoing techno-style beat, a taste of house-style music for irregular progressions, and unique rhythms, Ambient Electronica has soft melodies and calming sound effects. A few good choices to try are Aphex Twin, Brian Eno, The Orb, and Future Sound of London.

- When trying New Age/Tribal music there are many recordings to choose from. The sound of this style is similar to Ambient Electronica, but unique non-electronic instruments like the harpsichord, chimes, bells, and didgeridoos are used. The beat is often similar to that of a drum circle and sometimes involves guttural throat sounds and chants.

- If you'd prefer to stay away from music, there is always non-musical sound effect CDs or tapes. These often feature babbling brooks, waves, rain, whale songs, waterfalls, and other sounds found in nature. If you are a city dweller that is having trouble sleeping because it is too quiet, there are recordings of city noises such as fire engines, traffic, and airplanes just for you.

- Sound machines are widely available and can be found at many different price points. Usually about the size of an alarm clock, they typically come with a selection of sounds to pick from. You can select how the recordings play, either as an ongoing loop or for a preset length of time. Some sound machines are even built into alarm clocks, and can be used to gently awaken you. When deciding which style of unit to purchase, keep in mind that the units that play synthesized sounds are best, because they most closely imitate the natural sound. The second choice is a sound device that only pays recorded samples.

The style of music that works best depends entirely on the individual. Some people respond better to non-linear music, while others find it easier to drift off to sleep with soothing percussion in the background. Some prefer random beats and tempo, others like a constant pattern of music. Try several different types to find the style that you prefer.

An interesting aside, music's relationship with sleep is the current focus of a study being conducted by the University of Toronto's psychiatry department and Toronto Western Hospital. In their sleep clinic, they are investigating "brain music". Brain music is EEG readings, converted to music via a computer program designed to compose customized music based on the EEG readings. Each sleeper's brain waves are watched and studied. The scientists determine which rhythmic and tonal sounds the individual is most responsive to and they input it into a computer. A computer program is used to develop a personalized "soundtrack" of music that will invoke the same brain wave patterns when the person is trying to fall asleep later. There is evidence that shows this personalized method of music therapy is highly effective. Obviously researchers are very interested in pursuing this method of relaxation since it is typically effective and does not involve possibly habit forming medication.

Reducing Your Evening Stimulation

The best nighttime routine is one that leaves you feeling relaxed and ready to go to bed. If you are experiencing trouble falling asleep, it may be beneficial to avoid external stimulations for an hour or so before bedtime. Stimulation, such as watching television, keeps your mind active and alert. If you find it difficult to give up television before bed, try to select shows that are calming rather than aggressive, action-packed programs.

When reducing your evening stimulation to promote healthy sleep habits, try these tips:

- Keep your bedroom television-free. This will help your mind and body associate the bedroom with sleeping only.

- Don't exercise up to three hours prior to bedtime. Remember that exercise wakes up your body, and unless physical activity is done well before you plan to go to bed, it will work against you when trying to sleep.

- Plan to unwind when returning home from being out. If you jump directly into bed, your mind and body might not have sufficient time to decompress and slip into your evening routine.
- Try reading. Non-technical reading might help make you tired. Avoid work-related or overly complicated material.
- Avoid falling asleep without turning off the light. This will wake you up in the night and disturb your sleep cycles, as well as you bedtime routine.

The goal is to define the fine line between stimulation and relaxation when deciding how to unwind. Being able to easily relax at night will be paramount to your success in falling asleep naturally.

Stay Away from Internal Stimulants

While there are many external stimulates in your environment, there are also stimulants that affect your body from the inside. Impacting the way you feel, think, and relax, these products contain caffeine, sugar, and chemicals. While you don't need to completely remove these items from your diet, you do need to pay attention and be sure not to ingest them after dinnertime to avoid difficulty falling asleep.

- Caffeinated beverages. Caffeine wakes up your body and mind by raising your heart rate. Since it has this effect, it is considered a stimulant. Coffee, colas, teas, and chocolate beverages contain caffeine. Have your last caffeinated beverage at least 3-4 hours prior to bedtime to avoid having difficulty sleeping.
- Chocolate. Chocolate has caffeine and sugar, both of which are stimulants that will keep you from having a restful night's sleep. Do not have chocolate for 2-3 hours prior to bedtime.
- Alcohol. While alcoholic beverages might make you feel tired and help you fall asleep, the sleep is typically not restful. For example, you might find yourself waking up in the middle of the night feeling dehydrated, then have trouble falling back to sleep. As with any other medication that can become addictive, you do not want to create a nightly dependency on alcohol to fall asleep at night.

- Smoking. Tobacco contains nicotine which is a stimulant. Your body's nicotine dependency can cause your body to wake when the level of nicotine in your blood becomes low. Try to not to smoke in the hours before bedtime.

Caffeine in Common Beverages and Drugs	
Beverages	
Brewed coffee, drip method, 5 oz cup	60-180 mg caffeine
Instant coffee, 5 oz. cup	30-120 mg caffeine
Decaffeinated coffee, 5 oz. cup	1-5 mg caffeine
Brewed tea, 5 oz. cup	60-180 mg caffeine
Instant tea, 5 oz. cup	25-50 mg caffeine
Iced Tea, 12 oz. cup	67-76 mg caffeine
Cola, 12 oz. cup	36-47 mg caffeine
Chocolate	
Dark/semisweet, 1 oz.	5-35 mg caffeine
Non-prescription Drugs	
Dexatrim	200 mg caffeine
No Doz	100 mg caffeine
Excedrin	65 mg caffeine

Your Diet Matters

Your diet impacts your ability to fall asleep and maintain sleep at night. By eating a healthy diet, low in processed foods, sugar, fat, and preservatives, you may find that you can stop the cycle of insomnia and improve your overall health.

Consider these guidelines for a healthy sleep diet:

- Follow the recommended daily guidelines for fruits and vegetables.
- Increase the complex carbohydrates in your diet.

- Eat protein that is low in fat, and consider meat substitutes like tofu or veggie burgers.
- Avoid spicy and heavy foods.
- If you need a snack before bed, make it low in fat and sugar.
- Eat you last meal four or more hours before bedtime.
- Try not to overeat at your nighttime meal because you might feel drowsy immediately after eating. Alternatively, be sure to eat enough so that you are not ravenous at bedtime.
- Drink plenty of water throughout the day. A well hydrated body won't wake up in the night because of dehydration. Drink eight glasses, equivalent to 2 liters of water per day.

Watch yourself for food allergies that might be subtly causing you sleep disturbances. Common food allergies that might affect your sleep patterns are wheat, dairy products, corn and chocolate.

A well-balanced, wholesome diet will help you be a healthier person overall. General health is a huge factor in your ability to fall asleep naturally. If your daily intake of food is healthy, your body and mind will be healthy and well-nourished, helping you sleep deeply without waking in the night.

Get Rid of Anxiety and Worry

Are you someone whose mind is filled with thoughts of your family, your finances, your job and the future, when you are trying to fall asleep? Do you find it hard to stop thinking and /or worrying about things long enough to drift off? If your mind is busy at bedtime, it can lead to constant tossing and turning and insomnia.

If you worry about situations in life, there are a few techniques you can use to help put the worry out of your mind, and fall asleep. First, realize that now is the time to sleep, and the situations and events that are causing you stress will be there tomorrow. Try making a "Worry Notebook." In a notebook designated for this purpose, create a list of what's causing you stress and anxiety before you go to bed. Then go through the list and identify which items can be dealt with tomorrow. The list of items on your list for tomorrow then becomes your to-do list for the next day. This will help you feel more in control and positive about situation.

In separate section of your notebook, create a list of things that you worry about but are out of your control. Reconfirm to yourself that you have no power to change these things.

When you have finished your lists, put away the notebook and remind yourself that you have put these things out of your mind, and onto paper, and will not think about them again until tomorrow. If you find yourself thinking about these stressors during the night, firmly remind yourself that you have put away the notebook until the morning and now is sleep time.

Another idea for getting rid of your worry and anxiety is to write in a diary daily. Along with a record of your day, be sure to include what bothers you and causes you stress. The main point of this exercise is to put your feelings on paper, thus releasing you from thinking and worrying about them at night.

For both of these techniques, the act of writing down your anxiety and worry, gives you permission to rest at night and handle your feelings the next day.

In addition to these techniques, consider using the relaxation tips detailed in the previous chapter. Yoga and soft music or relaxing sounds may help to clear your mind. Consider trying light reading to keep your mind off worrisome thoughts. If you teach your mind to relax, you will find it easier to achieve a night of restful sleep.

Bath time

A soothing warm bath an hour or so before bedtime will relax you and help you feel sleepy. Do not try to go to sleep immediately following the bath because warm water has a stimulating effect on your body by raising your body temperature. After the bath, you will probably find yourself getting drowsy as your body temperature returns to normal.

How does a warm bath help you sleep better? The warm water will relax your major muscle groups, help your circulatory system, and raise your body temperature. When your core temperature returns to normal about an hour after the bath, you'll still feel relaxed and comfortable and your body will be ready for sleep.

Creating a peaceful bath time experience is easy and enjoyable. To make a soothing bath environment, light candles and use dim lighting in the bathroom. Experiment with scented oils or incense. Put on some light, tranquil music, and enjoy the mellow environment.

Another way to make your bath special is to add herbs to the water. Make a blended herb to take advantage of the herb's relaxing qualities. Put the sachet in the tub when it's filling, and hold it under the hot water while it steeps. Unwind in the tub while enjoying the herbal scents. A few comforting herbs to try are lavender, chamomile, mint, passion flower, and lime flower.

There are many aromatic oils on the market that are created to induce relaxation. About 4-5 drops of the essential oil is added to the bath after the tub is filled. When deciding on an essential oil to use, try rose, chamomile, lavender, hops, ylang-ylang, vetiver, or neroli for a calming bath.

Bath powder is a third choice of enhancements that can be added to your bath. This recipe for bath powder should be added to the water while you are filling the tub.

Milk & Honey Bath Powder

½ cup honey

3 cups powdered milk

Lavender buds

Preparation

Mix all ingredients well in a large bowl. Add several tablespoons of the milk bath to warm water in the tub. Store any remaining mixture in a sealed container.

Bath time is a great way to encourage relaxation and drowsiness. Experiment with various herbs and oils to find the ones that work best for you.

Chapter 3
Herbal Remedies and Supplements

Your Body's Natural Hormones
Melatonin (chemically named 5-methoxy-N-acetyltryptamine) is a naturally occurring hormone in humans. The pineal gland, a tiny organ at the center of our brains, secretes melatonin at night to help our bodies maintain a sleep schedule.

The body's internal clock that tells us when to sleep and when to wake up is the body's circadian rhythm. This rhythm is regulated by melatonin.

Darkness encourages the pineal gland to release melatonin, while light represses the release of melatonin. Researchers have found that the pineal gland's release of, and the production of, melatonin decreases as we get older. This explains why young people typically have less sleep-related problems than older people.

Scientists have synthesized naturally occurring melatonin, and it is now available over-the-counter as a supplement. No prescription is needed, and the supplement is available in drug and health food stores in the United States.

Melatonin is not regulated by the Food and Drug Administration (FDA) or any other government agency. Since it is naturally occurring in some foods, the U.S. Dietary Supplement & Education Act of 1994 permits it to be available as a dietary supplement.

Melatonin is has proven to be successful when used to treat sleep problems. Two of the sleep situations most helped by melatonin supplementation are insomnia related to jet-lag and delayed sleep-phase disorders.

How much melatonin should you take? Each individual should begin with a small amount of melatonin (about 1 mg), and increase their dosage if needed. Melatonin comes in pill form and range most commonly from 1 mg to 3 mg.

When should you take melatonin? For maximum effectiveness, take melatonin about a half an hour prior to bed time. If you regularly sleep during the nighttime, you should not take melatonin during the day because it can impact your circadian rhythm. The opposite is true if you sleep during the day and work at night. If you want to prevent jet lag when traveling across many time zones, take a dose prior to flying and a second dose 30 minutes before going to bed.

As with any supplement, there are several issues to consider. Although melatonin has been used for a long time without problems or side effects, it is not FDA-approved, and is unregulated by any regulatory agency. Anything you ingest that is not FDA-approved does not have a seal of approval regarding the supplement's safety or purity, and the effectiveness of the product cannot be guaranteed. Another concern is the lack of study and information regarding interactions with other medicines.

Consult a doctor before taking melatonin if you have diabetes, a depressive disorder, an auto-immune disease, epilepsy, lymphoproliferative disorder, leukemia, or are taking an MAO inhibitor. This product should be used by adults only and is not for use by children, teens, or pregnant or breast-feeding women.

The Benefits of Chamomile

Matricaria camomilla, commonly called "Chamomile", is native to southern and central Europe. This flowering plant is now widely grown in the United States, Argentina, Australia, Egypt and northern Africa. The leaves and flowers are dried and used as tea, either in teabags or in loose tea form.

For centuries, chamomile has been used as a sleep-promoting supplement. One of the benefits of using chamomile as a sleep aid is that it does not need to be taken over a long period of time to be effective. Chamomile can be used to treat anxiety and insomnia on the spot.

There are a few ways to use chamomile. It can be placed in a sachet under the pillow. Try brewing a tea and drink it 30-45 minutes prior to going to sleep. Chamomile is most effective in treating transient (or mild) insomnia.

The naturally occurring chemical in chamomile that promotes drowsiness and encourages sleep is called chrysin. Chrysin is also found in passion flower (Passiflora incarnates), which is another herbal sleep aid and anxiety reducer.

If you find your insomnia is due to congestion and/or allergies, chamomile works as anti-histamine to reduce swelling from allergies and help you sleep better. However, chamomile can create a similar allergic reaction to that of ragweed and other plants in the same family like aster or chrysanthemum. Avoid taking chamomile if you have these allergies.

Chamomile Tea Recipe (one serving)

1 cup water

1 teaspoon dried chamomile flowers

lemon juice

honey

Preparation

Add the chamomile to boiling water either using a tea infuser or directly into the water. Cover and boil for 35-40 seconds. Remove the saucepan from the heat and let the tea steep for one minute. If using loose tea, remove with a strainer. Serve with honey and a twist of lemon. For an added calming effect, use a few leaves of Lemon Balm, also called Melissa officinalis, instead of the lemon juice.

The Soothing Properties of Lavender

Lavender originated in the western Mediterranean and Arabians are believed to have been the first to domesticate the flowering shrubbery. The Romans later spread the growing and cultivation of the plant across Europe. The Pilgrims brought lavender to America. Lavender was also one of the first plants brought to Australia in the 1800's.

Many herb gardens contain garden grown or container grown lavender. Lavender is grown in somewhat alkaline soil, in a sunny location with good drainage.

Lavender's essential oils act as a tranquilizer to calm the central nervous system, making it highly effective as an herbal remedy for insomnia. The dried flowers and leaves can be brewed and drunk in a tea, or the plant's essential oils can be extracted from the plant. Essential oils can be applied to the skin as a muscle relaxant, or the scent can be inhaled as used in aromatherapy. Since the feet are know as an area of the body that quickly absorbs topically applied products, massaging lavender oil into the feet will have a calming effect. The essential oil can be vaporized in a vaporizer or added to a warm bath and inhaled. You can also create a sachet of the dried leaves and flowers, sprinkle with essential lavender oil, and slip it under your pillow.

Some people who apply lavender topically have experienced an allergic reaction when the oil contacts the skin. Always conduct an allergy test on a small patch of skin to test for sensitivity prior to using a full application.

It's also important to note that not all lavender species have the same calming effects. Spanish lavender, for example, is used to invigorate and wake up the body.

Lavender & Mint Tea (one serving)

1 teaspoon fresh lavender flowers (or ½ teaspoon dried)

1 ½ - 2 tablespoons fresh mint leaves (or 2 teaspoons dried)

1 cup water

Other herbs like rosemary, lemon balm or lemon verbena, or rose geranium for added flavor

Preparation

Using a teapot, mix the lavender and mint. You can use a tea infuser or simply add the loose leaves and strain it later. Add boiling water and let it steep for five minutes.

Handmade Lavender Sachet

Dried or fresh lavender

Lavender oil

A cloth or handkerchief

1 large needle to fit a ribbon, 1 regular sized needle

Thread, ¼" wide ribbon

Preparation

1. Prepare your handkerchief by folding in half, then folding in half a second time, creating a pouch. If you prefer a crisp look, iron the edges.
2. Using the threaded needle, sew three of the four sides.
3. Fill the pouch with lavender through the unsown side. Use enough of the lavender to fill the pouch, but don't overstuff it. The final product will resemble a bean bag. Add approximately 8-10 drops of essential oil to the dried lavender.
4. With the larger needle threaded with ribbon, loosely sew the open side to keep all of the sachet contents inside.
5. When sealed, knot the ribbon and enjoy your homemade sachet!

The Medicinal Use of Valerian Root

Valeriana officinalis, otherwise known as "Valerian Root", is considered to be one of the most effective natural remedies available for insomnia. The see the benefits of valerian root, the herb must be taken regularly over a period of about one month to see results. After taking valerian root for about a month, you will find that it encourages relaxation and deep sleep.

Valerian root flowers late in the spring, and it is typically found in pastures and heath land in the wild. The rhizomes and roots are the parts of the plant that are used for most herbal remedies. Most often the valerian root is collected in September and dried to make widely available herbal products.

At Switzerland's Nestle Research Laboratories, researchers P.D. Leatherwood, Ph.D., and F. Chauffard, Ph.D., determined that the efficacious dose of valerian as a sleep aid is 450 mg. Higher doses cause grogginess without being more effective. Leatherwood also found in a separate study that valerian root was not only effective as a relaxant, but also improved the quality of sleep.

It is understood that valerian root's impact on the body is similar to that of benzodiazepine, an ingredient in Valium™. One of the advantages of valerian root over other sedatives is that there is not next day cloudiness or grogginess. It has been said that Valium's name came from valerian root, but it's important to note that they are chemically completely different and should not be considered to be related.

Prescribed sleep aids can be toxic, however, valerian root is non-toxic and does not hinder the ability to drive nor does it negatively interact with alcohol. Valerian root is used to provide relief from anxiety disorders, and acts as a sedative to encourage restful sleep.

Herbalists sometime recommend taking fresh valerian root over the extract because of the possibility of a delayed stimulant effect on some people. Depending on your body chemistry, valerian root sometimes causes an initial sedative effect, then several hours later provides an energy surge, obviously not a desirable trait when taken as a sleep aid. The fresh valerian root is less likely cause a delayed stimulant effect.

A World of Other Herbs

Kava

Piper methysticum, also called "Kava", is found mainly in Samoa and Tonga in western Polynesia, as well as most of Melanesia and in Micronesia. This shrub is part of the pepper family (Piperaceae).

Kava is widely available in health food stores and comes in several forms. It's used as an on-the-spot treatment for anxiety. Most popular is the kava extract, which is available in a convenient spray that can be kept handy for a quick spritz under the tongue when in need of immediate anxiety relief. Raw kava is also available, but it is recommended to purchase the high grade lateral root for best results.

Professional herbalists say that kava's effective daily dose is between 70 and 200 mg of kavalactones. Kavalactones are major active components of kava that have the psychoactive impact. The best dose to encourage a restful night's sleep is 150-200 mg, taken about 20-30 minutes before going to sleep.

Lemon Balm

Melissa officianalis, commonly known as "Lemon Balm", has an enjoyable lemon flavor, and is often used in a relaxing and tasty tea.

Found mainly in northern Africa and southern Europe, this perennial herb is part of the mint family. It can be grown in an herb garden with well-drained soil, and lemon balm does well in sandy soil with full sun.

Try a lemon balm tea by adding 2 teaspoons dried lemon balm to 1 cup of boiling water. Brew the tea for 10 minutes and drink immediately before bedtime.

Passion Flower

Passaflora incarnate, also known as "passion flower", is often used as a relaxant, and is taken to calm the muscles and digestive system, and aid in digestion. It is taken in tea form.

Passion flower grows in the southern US and Latin America, and is also known by its folk names Passion Vine and Maypops. Throughout history passion flower has been used as a substitute for tobacco and as a tranquilizer.

Some herbalists consider passion flower to be the best herbal remedy for treating intransigent insomnia. Passion flower is not addictive and provides relief from sleeplessness. There are no known side effects, and passion flower can be used by the elderly and children without concern.

Dried passion flower makes a highly effective tea. To brew passion flower tea, steep 1 teaspoon of dried herb in one cup of boiling water for 15 minutes. Drink tea 30 minutes before bed time.

California Poppy

Eschscholtzia californica, commonly called "California poppy" contains protopine. Protopine has a similar effect as morphine on the brain. The California poppy does not have the same narcotic as its sister the Opium poppy, although there is a resemblance in its structure. California poppy is not addictive. Scientists have not actively studied the effects of California poppy so there are no guidelines for dosage.

Hops

Humulus lupulus, also known as "hops", are the main flavoring ingredient in beer. Hops are the strobiles, or fruit, of the plant. The hops plant is a member of the cannibis family. Hops are usually used in conjunction with other herbs when being used for its sedative qualities, although it can be effectively used on its own as well. Hops come as dried stobiles, capsules, and tablets, and are commonly used as a relaxing tea or as a sachet placed underneath the pillow.

To make a sachet, follow the previously given lavender sachet instructions, only replace the lavender with a mixture of ¼ cup hop stobiles, 1/8 cup chamomile flowers, and 1/8 cup lavender. Sprinkle with lavender oil and sew open side. Enjoy the calming scents provided by your new sachet.

Honey

Try mixing honey into warmed milk or herbal teas to benefit from its sedating qualities. Add one teaspoon honey and one drop vanilla extract to a cup of warm milk and enjoy immediately before going to sleep.

Vitamin & Mineral Supplements

By adding vitamins and minerals to your balanced diet, you might find relief from sleeplessness. Many people are not getting enough of certain vitamins and minerals that are needed for sleeping well. One of these nutritional supplements may help:

- Calcium. Too little calcium in your diet can cause the inability to sleep. Combine a daily 600mg supplement with food for the best effect.

- Magnesium. A deficiency in magnesium can cause nervousness resulting in shallow sleeping and the inability to stay asleep. A supplement of 250g taken daily, or the addition of magnesium-rich foods such as almonds, kelp and wheat bran can help.

- Vitamin B-6 (pyridoxine). Vitamin B-6 is needed to produce the levels of serotonin required by the body to trigger sleep. The recommended dosage of B-6 is 50-100mg daily, and can be taken in nutritional yeast form and mixed into a glass of fruit juice.

- Vitamin B-12 (cobalamin). If you don't get enough B-12, you may experience grogginess, confusion, or memory loss, and insomnia. B-12 is often combined with B-5, and is found naturally in wheat germ, bananas, peanuts and sunflower seeds. If taken as a supplement, the recommended dosage is 25mg per day.
- Vitamin B-5 (pantothenic acid). Too little B-5 can cause insomnia and tiredness. Vitamin B-5 works as an anxiety reducer, and a daily dose of 100mg is recommended.
- Folic acid. The synthetic supplement of folic acid is processed by the body more effectively than folic acid found in nature. Too little folic acid can cause insomnia. Foods containing folic acid include leafy roughage, orange juice, beans and fortified breakfast cereal. The recommended dosage is 400mg per day.
- Copper. According to a recent study, pre-menopausal women with a deficiency in copper commonly have difficulty falling asleep. In this study, women taking 2mg of copper daily fell asleep quicker and felt more refreshed when waking. A good way to include more copper in your diet is by eating cooked oysters and lobster.

A balanced diet is the best way to combat vitamin deficiencies. You can try adding a few supplements to see if you notice a substantial difference. If you do not see a notable change, stop supplementing and focus of eating well and exercising regularly.

Conclusion

This book has provided you with a number of ways to fight sleep problems naturally, without relying on harmful or potentially addicting narcotics or other medications. When trying these alternative methods, test a couple at a time so that you can more easily identify what works well for you, and what doesn't. Select methods that you can commit to and apply right away.

As with any medical concern, don't hesitate to contact your doctor to discuss your sleep problems and determine if your symptoms may be related to your general health. Your physician can guide you through traditional channels, as well as the natural remedies detailed in the book. The main priorities are handling your sleep-related problems, and protecting your overall health.

Made in United States
Orlando, FL
04 April 2025